BAPTISM

LAUREN CROWLEY

Copyright © 2016 by Lauren Crowley

All rights reserved. No part of this book may be used or reproduced in any manner whatsoever without written permission except in the case of brief quotations embodied in critical articles and reviews.

First paperback edition published in 2016 by Crowley Press
CrowleyPress.com

Printed in the United States of America

Library of Congress Cataloging-in-Publication Data
ISBN: 978-0-9982322-0-1
1. Poetry 2. Spirituality 3. New Age 4. Metaphysical

to the inexpressible gold and those that help me feel it

table of contents

Part I		1
Part II		99

Part I

we made a home in the flowers, they speak of the stars, and how we unfolded, descended, down onto earth, a plan, we had a plan, a twinkle in our eye, all along, the joy of remembering, the strength of putting into place. sometimes it is small. big to us, though. reach your hand out - it's just over there. create a list. if you only had so much time, what would you cherish. what will you come back for if you forget?

we are a girl of the flowers, a woman of the dirt. when i talk to the rocks they sigh in relief, under my feet. no one ever hears them. it is time to trust things much older than us.

my older sister gave me four dragons, breath abated, they wait. because they knew me before, when i was like them - don't you see, those days we were free. i tried to talk about the garden of eden but i have this curious feeling that i am the only one with eyes wide open. they say breathe it in - the sediment will cure you.

i, too, am layered red and brown. and i will always remember. their hands, they clutch at my ankles, when we reset they show me. you were here, you were here - a million miles away. some people don't even believe. i would show them the photographs, the album of my own making, if it was in my hands, and not my mind.

we are many. we've said it before, we'll say it again. and when we are buried, we will be one. only one name written on the stone, but it will breathe the others. in whispers. and layers in you will remember, too.

(a field of flowers, each bud a promise, a dream)

(july 26, 2016)

My eyes blink as I remember the days, we were longing, we were threadbare, my heart beat hard on the ground. We didn't care when our clothes got dirty, we were one with what we were. I thought it made sense at the time. It did.

But something swept me up, that old spaceship, transported me elsewhere. Places are feelings, and I'm not much else than a collection of inklings.

Never could pick a favorite color. When I was seven it was green, when I was eight it was yellow, when I was nine it was a purplish grey. Wouldn't it be nice to have a destination, a clue - but I think we have one. It is a feeling.

I'm twenty-four and it's gold.

Seven pm in the summer gold. Wishing on a dandelion gold, light, lightly. The Golden Age - that is our wish, don't spoil it, I'm keeping secrets again, but this time they're made of hope and not shame.

We have all the cards in our hands, and so we put the tarot cards away. A witch doesn't need a crystal ball, it's all written in her soul. I'll help you piece it out, I am no translator, but a prodder. The woman holding the torch in the dark.

Lion's heart, don't forget your own kingdom. Who lives there, but your own cells, your dreams, your heart. There is nothing more important. At least not now. Go there - and return. We must always return, and find the kingdom on earth.

And Pan will help, and we will sing, and forces unknown to us will coalesce, until we no longer coagulate, but bleed out. We will wash away on a river of our own blood - Listen to it. Listen to me, and then forget what I've said. Only you have the map, cover your ears, and Listen hard.

(july 27, 2016)

Baptism

we wade out into the bigger something -
this is the farthest we've ever gone
precipice of sand, what lurks beneath,
what waves will hit me and push me below,
water in my nose,
but we can't return to the shore
and we mustn't
and we wouldn't
if we could

(july 28, 2016)

Let the honey ooze out the wound

I'm ripe, I'm wild

(july 29, 2016)

Baptism

it comes in waves, doesn't it, but what about when we're dry?
prostrate on the floor, someone else's floor,
prostrate looking for the door, the gate to heaven,
inside this pisces mind, virgo's got me clipping my nails
until we've had enough, sink down low, slow,

in a dream we cast a circle,
my mother, my aunt - two scorpio souls
and a baby lamb would not let it close
I said 'it needs space' and my mom frowned,
when we finished our divination I needed time,
I never leave this place without going to the other,
the indigo place, Heal me Encircle me,
you've been here all along

(You! you!)

we're two

(july 29, 2016)

Crowley

I am a dancer, spinning past the things you thought were mine,
no, they never were, just because the mind grasps them doesn't mean
the heart will submit, I'm tip-toeing on my own idle leisure, as if I can't
lay myself down, she lays down, she sighs into the mist,
we're in the midst of this, friends with the waiting,
worried about the words we cannot spare

don't open up the cocoon before it's set in,
there is more to it, the space in between seems mean
but it isn't

(july 29, 2016)

Baptism

we've been feeling Angelic, as if we came from the star herself, as if we remember,
although there's much below, we can lift our hands on high, bless these fingers,
bless my mind. Each kiss from me to you a blessing, douse us in holy water.
put out the flames, we've quit playing with matches, now the Sun fuels our fire
and we are warm. Let us be clear, because these veins get icy, infused with alien
memories, starry-eyed still we rise, in the moment you became my worldly brother,
we were planted here like feathers, we were brought here on a hunch, in a dream
my friends were turning blue and you fought them, I didn't mind, but we too turn blue
when we lay under the Moon

Just taste me, too, molasses and youth

(july 29, 2016)

Crowley

In a Red Room, vines curling down the wall black and white tile, a place of permission, destiny, fate, focus - no time, open the windows wide and let the light hit your chest, engulf it, envision - trust. Trust all that is, you are here, you are divine. Trust in the steps you take, as they are never wrong, only wobbling, don't stop walking, not until you find the pond. when you swim inside yourself you will be covered in it, this is our Baptism.

(july 29, 2016)

Baptism

and we are unique, the ink in our nails drew only the priestess, the alien, the calm
we never could explain what we meant,
we only knew how it made us shake,
how when we talked to our guide the room filled with blue,
and we Knew, we Knew

Almost drew on my skin- Heretic
but it was something else, wasn't it

our own divine
Prayer, pollination
Performing the rites

this was our sacred rebellion,

just as Lilith left Adam's side,
and laid down with an angel

(july 29, 2016)

Samael, Samael, bring me back whence I came,
enjoy me, share in me, all that I am,
as if their hands never... as if
the first time my eyes opened
I was under the Red Sea,
and I swam to the surface,
and you pulled me out,
the first woman was never
an infant, only a threat,
claws and wings,
your favorite things,

(july 29, 2016)

Baptism

always feeling from the outside, we put our hands under the waterfall but it's scalding hot, it's all for naught, we weren't meant to follow the road lined with bones, leave my carcass there and you will find a golden locket, with my love's picture inside, leave me there and my ghost will whisper these words, they've been replaying in my head, like a song someone sings, a woman who lives alone, haunted minds haunted homes, will you smell my sweet grass oil or will my body give off a perfume of its own -

the wasp lives in the chandelier. and we bathe below it.

(july 29, 2016)

Crowley

a house on a hill, sepia, wind - snakes live inside but we don't know why, a woman lives inside and from a crystal ball she divines, but when you're deep in your core what could the future tell? she sees past your words, she sees only soul -

what do we birth in isolation, but a painful and messy child. let it run loose, let it run wild.

(july 29, 2016)

Baptism

two thumb prints in my cushion-heart of lyrical fancy

let me stand alone - each feathered wing gifted from the glory above

what are they made of -

the chattering of my chest, messages from home (lightyears away, lamp-light)
love letters, dust bunnies guarding treasured belongings, my soul's longing

truth, the kind that sparkles, the constellations led us to the inner dwelling, and now we have no need for the sky,

we know what we would regret if we gave it up,
we know what our heart sings for,
there's nothing else on the table,
only a pair of keys

(july 29, 2016)

Crowley

I am cultivating - this is a cult of my own making,
yellow roses, dandelion floor, feed me to the peaches,
we'll always want more - see me to the dark patches
in the well-lit wood, where the fauns will catch me
and remind me of the good,

just as Pan once pulled me
out of a frost-bit mood,
the seeds are for sowing,
aroused, understood

(july 29, 2016)

Baptism

Faithless, I walked upon thorns, until I stood bleeding, with open arms

(july 30, 2016)

when we crossed the path of the Sun we made some sacrifices, we came cold-blooded, we sought out home in graceful hands, your hands, mine, soft sifting rhymes, summer time, somewhere we'll find, answers the philosophers dreamt up slowly, the flesh is instant, pleasure is pressing, and to think we almost forgot, somewhere inside we're still hot, hereditary, milkweed from the stars - kiss me and you'll see

(july 30, 2016)

Baptism

the vestal virgins slink down my ribcage as if there's something to protect, insides trembling, ready to melt, combust, forget - part our lips and give one hint, my body's a terrarium blooming something new, a city, a foreign land, we're giving birth to a civilization, and it's the golden age, a science fiction utopia a girl of peace, we built over the desolation, you see each time we lamented the seeds fell from our eyes, protruding, dissolution, buried in the ground. and the trees will grow green, strong, singing, our myth begins now,

and one day the scholars will speak of the primordial times, where was Athena before she escaped from her father's head, but in the shadow of an orderly world

(july 30, 2016)

midnight paths take me to the place where I will wake up - dust my eyelashes with early morning dew and sunlit cocoons, I've missed this

a blanket made of this moment - as if the adventure is now, here, living and breathing, constantly, cursively,

freedom, freedom to leave, take a few steps away from the family pond, dip my hands in cool waters, untouched, promise. promise.

pleasantries are no longer pleasant and the wild beast can't be tamed, set me free so that things will fall into place, saw-dust, brush it away, we'll gut the interior and make room for the moon, my cocoon, marked: anew anew anew

(july 31, 2016)

Baptism

I saw myself in white frills, too feminine for my own good, cabins, woods. I hug innocence like the lover I left behind. We're always bursting beyond the seams like we've come with two, three suitcases to peruse, hand-me-downs, my memory my muse, identities shift and confuse, each dress a different hue, follow me back you've got nothing to lose.

but I'll trail that red string behind me, I've time-traveled before and I mustn't lose my center of gravity, pull me closer, love, and tell me you have me - like before, sleepily, lay me down to rest in clothes that were sewn for me

(august 1, 2016)

what do we fill the empty spaces up with, but gold-stripped butterflies looming, mystery over uncertainty, a maenad's chant to the morning like we've never seen any of this before, I want to wake up plush, pining - prepared for what is to come, in the afternoon we're praying, my skin melted away like rose-water in the air and now there's nothing left but Sunday communion - sweet on my tongue, more like honey than bread. we were divine all along,

especially when we wouldn't part our lips for the songs, totally vacant for the psalms there was no one present but my body and my God

only Mary listened and she saw - I draped myself in blue and stood sacrosanct, they thought I threw the baby out with the bathwater but that's not true

(august 1, 2016)

Baptism

songstress breathing fog against the window, this wind's bringing in a current of love, we're reading about belief and the power of the heart, teach me, so that I may become. there was something written long ago and we will fulfill this covenant, what do they call it, dharma, how do we say it, fate - star-crossed lovers, craftsman carving wood. me, opening up to you.

and the blood from the tip of my fingers, something spilling out, it's in my hair it's in my doubt, the quest, the cause - always, forever, purpose and place, let it blossom out, give yourself to it, they say, throw yourself in the ocean of your love. two sides of the same roman coin, my poetry my partner. we were born a rose, we are a candle ever-lit, fragrant - the scent you're always searching for

(august 1, 2016)

Crowley

And now I Align

it's not lightening striking my skull it's soiled hands grabbing Zeus's only threat, God's only prohibition, they made us in their image and they were rebels, too, nothing to tempt like Saturn's only restriction, they made Prometheus with loving hands and they kissed Lucifer's forehead as they pushed him over, the, edge,

good Luck, son,

you'll need some guile to light up the whole world

(august 1, 2016)

Baptism

read my palms and what will you find but finely-etched grooves, they told me this one would bring love and so I made it deeper, taking a knife to my heavenly composition, creation happens every time we close our eyes and imagine, now imagine this:

you can have it all, don't hold your ear up against the wall listening to the absolutes of prophets and preachers, hold your hand against your heart the auricle is your oracle there is no more seeking, only knowing, and acting accordingly. believe it and let it be

so that when we curl up in our grave we are quiet, cozy, riddled with stories, we will share them with our sisters, they are waiting from afar, watching from the stars, this life is ours -

"I want life to be like a movie you don't want to finish, y'know?"

(august 1, 2016)

Crowley

I wanted to flee to the desert I wanted to get away, become one with the Sun and the dirt, I wanted this for myself and more, mystery, the things only the hot earth speaks, I thought I would find something, my wings, the vines cut away from my arms (save me) we were born to be sovereign, golden queen, hot tears, madness in the middle of the mojave please, set me free. please, please, please.

I won't please you anymore. Washing my hands of this and screaming you out of my soul, unleash the fury, the fugue. If this is an illusion I'm blinking my eyes

Athena didn't have a mother, she had a sword and a shield

(august 1, 2016)

Baptism

cradle me in something warm, swaddle me, gently push your fingers into my chest until I'm intoxicated on something other than my own thoughts, don't we envy the animals, for they do not part ways with their truth, mine left when fear arose and so let it fall away, let us vanquish it, phantoms in the night, we are moving into a new body, one made of light, it's why your stomach hurts, it's why you sleep so deeply, we are changing.

protect what we have, a packet of seeds, a garden just planted. no one can take this away from me. written in the stars, there's no need to struggle, there's only breathing out, put your lips to the grave, count the beads for each self we have lost, they can be put to rest, for we no longer need them.

let the king take their place, he will govern and he will save. as if we were heathens for the chains, we need a new religion. bible made of flesh, blood, leaves - a beating heart. cast away your sins, there is only one: self-denial. pressed against the wall we lie, we lie all the time, think we're hidden away, you cannot hide it. don't extinguish the flame, please, oh please, think wisely, think of what you're doing.

the ember will keep burning, child, let it erase you, encase you, holy. holy. holy.

(august 2, 2016)

A bird flew into the kitchen (song-bird) and we wouldn't let it get away, cupped it in our hands, we took a break from the cleaning and we set our mind astray, landed on a branch of our own making, and I'm taken, what was once just a fancy is now an obsession, a passion, a purpose.

(august 2, 2016)

Baptism

just because we reach back into the misery pit does not mean we are still there. just because we are healing does not mean we are still broken. memories or nightmares, my heart has burn marks, wash them away, cleanse me, our love brings renewal, sadness can be sweet and don't let them take that away, we walked over mountains and through brumble bush just pick out the thorns, open your eyes to what is, this moment, a new story is written

(august 2, 2016)

something called me, and I became a martyr for it. you know how I plunge -

(august 3, 2016)

Baptism

we wondered which women were like us, could we line up our faces next to theirs, our words next to theirs, our pain next to theirs, to make sense of it all, as if I need a reference point, as if I could not create something new

(august 3, 2016)

still sniffing the flowers of July, something took form, a mirage lowering upon me as my fingers fell through sand - we were afraid of blossoms in the desert because we could not lick the hot dirt, we wanted something we could taste, something only a little bit tart. we were it, we heard the song and it was the one we were waiting for all along,

in certainty I saw a parallel life - one that was always golden, and it was always waiting for me to merge with it, mirror it, become it. that is bliss, aligning

(august 3, 2016)

Baptism

you can treat the invisible with the invisible

the corpse flower bloomed and in a tidy room I did too
did you know primal and pristine mean the same thing?

as my soul went on sojourn it decided to part ways with
thoughts, the only thing between me and the gold glow

we've returned now, resolute. knowing. astute.

(we let the heart out, it tumbled from my mouth,
easier to confess my sins than to let go of my doubt)

(august 4, 2016)

in a dream I was sure, in the smallest crevice of my soul I am, too,
something far away, unconstructed, I didn't make it with my hands,
it made its way out of me, the origin, arranged, starlight star bright,
who's the one you'll dream of tonight

give me the peace that only death brings, give it to me now,
for I shall live lightly, composed, all of those things we hold
tightly, we will let go

(august 4, 2016)

Baptism

these are the past lives I didn't see,
a shadow of me, written between the lines in my
palms I lap the chocolate-dark milk from my cup and
I will go on -

are we a dweller in the valley tonight, oasis flows through me,
follow me, I dipped my finger tips in holy water once and now
I plunge my hands in, it's all mine, it's all mine, see how the
blood washes off...

Fullness, finally - molting as I melt away, all that stood in my way,
I am heavy with it, never knew the first twenty-four years was just a
gestation,

let my life be a gesture,
generous in my demonstration
- Fertile.

(august 5, 2016)

like I had been a Demiurge all along, giantess breaking through the sea
and let the details drip off of me, solemn, funeral for my smallness,
stop me, I dare you, but you can't - fateful, even your god is on my side,
conceptual, laying the blueprints so the blue eyes of my youth will shine
forth, remarkable, isn't it, the flood that pours from my wounds

(august 5, 2016)

Baptism

an alien agenda walking around, two legs, two arms,
no wonder we hid it away, I saw my eyes in the mirror and I was
safe, I pray to the angels please protect me, they said protect yourself

blue, blue, blue
there is power in you, too

(Empress, oh Empress, telephone soon, we need your old wisdom,
we'd like to play your tune)

(august 5, 2016)

Crowley

What do I hold in my hands but rocks - I will throw each one into the river
each one with a name, a face, a place, a pain

I will throw each one in until there is nothing left
but the things too big to throw, I stand upon them,
and I Know

(august 5, 2016)

Baptism

I was once nothing but a lover-
until I found out I was an artist
and now I see they are the same thing

(august 5, 2016)

aren't we glad people paint pictures of flowers,
portrait of all that we seek

(august 5, 2016)

Baptism

DIANA LUCIFERA,
one in the same,
glowing, growing,
halcyon, too,

a hymn for my hope
though it was buried
in the well out back
we carried it with us
discretely, secretly

serene Selene,
settle into me
make life easy
luminary,
womb

(august 5, 2016)

first I must be a girl -

This is my essence. It always has been. Nymph in the woods, speaking to the flowers because they are the same species, I am this, I am pleasure laid out under a tree, breeze, open your mouth, stick out your tongue, and let god drip the honey, amply, lavish me, lascivious and innocent, I am what comes from the earth when you love it

(august 5, 2016)

Baptism

and oh if we could let her out, we've protected her from the world for the world is cruel, gazing, adjusting, shaming - what came from my utmost innocence is by some called evil

(august 5, 2016)

Crowley

swimming pools at night, fairy lights, who comes to me when I'm curled up in bed, blues whites reds, I would like to thank my guardian angel, for being there even when I can't see. even when I didn't believe

did they teach me to heal? if not them, me, I cracked apart once, and I learned to fight, I fell apart once, and sometimes I still do, old patterns, old waves, new ocean, new sky

I'm playing this life by ear, someone's humming in my heart, and I finally learned to listen. I'll teach this to you.

(august 5, 2016)

Baptism

all we have left is the locket, our two pounds of gold, and though we don't see them the butterflies inside, we sold our possessions and now we're possessed, solely, by this notion, affectivity, frivolous thinking, sometimes we're the wife in the haunted house, the wife no one believes, but we must be patient with those that keep their attic doors closed, yes we are like an animal or a child, the stars in our eyes fall out and we can't collect them all at once,

credibility, how often do we stand on trial one inch from the asylum, we don't have answers to their questions, because how can we explain life. how do we explain angels?

(august 7, 2016)

Crowley

we held a seance for the parts that are gone, in a circle we sat, in a circle we roam,

held out my hand to whomever would come, inviting it back, inviting it home

strong enough to feel, strong enough to let go

(august 7, 2016)

Baptism

let this be a hideaway, a home, lord knows we need it, always wondering what to divulge, we're full of secrets, big ones, whales under the moon, I'm seeing now how much I really want you, I'm feeling now how easily I could hold you, there is power in that, in the way rainbows seem mighty and rain calms us down

destiny is easy, destiny isn't hard

(august 7, 2016)

Crowley

our reveries are filled with green watercolors, velvet furniture, warm windows
harps - harmless things, encircle my wrists like a red string, pull me back to you

I was thirteen and I found a dead snake, I collected the bones, I kept them, and then I buried them

They weren't mine to keep

(and then I met you)

(august 8, 2016)

Baptism

Mother Mary's tears were heavier, hotter,

the crone said we wouldn't be raw forever
but the water-level's rising,

the tears my body my brain are one in the ocean
raise me up, I am breathing. beating, besotted

filled to the brim, heavy, hot

a flash flood gives me away,
you can't contain the primordial sea for long

nothing's wrong, it's just echolocation

mapping the difference

and every day the ocean gets wider
Saturn makes real what Neptune already sees

(august 8, 2016)

all we're doing is clearing the clutter from the doorway. Widening it, tearing down the walls, hanging welcome signs, and waiting, hands clasped like we're praying

(august 8, 2016)

Baptism

there is much to be learned from these unruly children,
hold them in your palm, as the scrapes on their knees bleed between your fingers
they cry for chaos they speak of a time when your world was held by a string,
the string between two people, your parents,
no earthquakes split the ground beneath you but you spent the night splitting your skull,
and you still do

you can't get away when you're the epicenter,
fault lines through your stomach laid on the floor for him to see

we pray he won't find it it hurts but we'll hide it

(august 9, 2016)

shall we enter the forest again, we've been laying in the grass flirting with the sun, but what of the dark secrets we stumble upon when we explore that mossy green? let's dig our hands into wet earth, the faeries have been waiting, they pushed me out the womb and they have a stake in this, too. I will return. mother of the promised land, sister of the dragon spirits and priestess of the moon, promise us this: remember the heartland never disown the weird, unyielding you are, fearsome you'll become, the blood never stops pulsating through stained-glass windows I was seconds away from my funeral in a dream and for once I was afraid,

remember the cult of Life there is justice in living, in grasping its hair like you cling to the oldest oak, looking for our mothers, looking for our right.... the rites of spring passed and we're still wondering if we belong. alien ears, sorceress tongue

(august 9, 2016)

Baptism

in the grand cathedral of our own shining belief, the grand alchemist, myself, my home. I will sit here in silence. I will share in what my spirit has always decided, it's way ahead of me, always, turning corners while I feel blind, blighted, let me be one with it, with the parts of me living elsewhere, beyond, I'm tired of being alone

(august 9, 2016)

Crowley

let me place, lovingly, this shattered ruin on the alter
we won't banish it to the corner anymore
no more pulling apart

because what can we pull from the wreckage
if not the reddest of roses,
passionate,
protective -

make jealousy my virtue,
not my foe

care to admit, care to supplant,
don't let it redden your cheeks,
lest you throw yourself overboard

(august 9, 2016)

Baptism

my anchor, yes,
pull me down lower,
until I'm buried half deep
you see, I'm safer that way
held by something stronger
solid, unto me, raving, the walls around me
notice these, the walls around my heart
and break them

so that the inevitable will ooze out

we're both afraid of spiders but
I'm not afraid of you

(august 10, 2016)

snow flurries of buttercup butterflies under the noon day sun,
I'm opening the windows to let happiness in
born on a Wednesday, brought into the world
casually, no, carefully, yes, a well-thought out plan
but we mustn't think much now, the soft sweet glory
will take us in, and show us the treasure trove

daydreams, dark shade, peace amongst the posies,
petals soft as silk, and laughing

(august 10, 2016)

Baptism

Taurus in the summer oozing dripping velveteen balmy breeze,
lay in the dirt and become nothing
but the bird singing

(august 10, 2016)

Crowley

I pine for the mother I will one day be, ink-stained hands touching curled locks of hair, stories and stories and stories beneath her feet, bones made of words, the words you are reading, the words of her soul. Confident in her choices, the silk worms make her clothes and the rabbits warm the hearth, she is Hestia, Vesta, voluntary relapse into an artist's madness, a painter's life. we grew from the cherub's wings, and we took form, the constellations wrote the script and we became the award-winning actress, no one could play the part but me

(august 10, 2016)

Baptism

I will be a better mother now that I'm a witch

I will be a better lover now that I'm a witch

(august 10, 2016)

Eros,
Apollo,
Erato,
come follow me on this path,
give me the wings and I'll give you the words,
we'll work together to untie this bow of fate,
purposeful, pleasing,
please imbue me with all that I'll be

(august 10, 2016)

Baptism

this is the seduction of a soul, let it emerge from its dark cave unadorned, wings pulled back we won't know its true form

(august 11, 2016)

we are a bound book of collected phrases,
words in pairs, better together, Venus weaves
her ribbon around us, them, whomever, makes
peace, between shining stars, never nameless,
always waiting, twins in the sky, twins in the air,
the temple, the wish, the beast also tamed,
was it the infinity of a maiden's mind or her
soft, strong hands

we went looking for poetry and only found
children, two, we drove home and we saw dogs,
in twos (we're two), swans dipping necks, is this
grace? closing our weary eyes in god's cloud cradle,
you are

buttermilk rising,
I took a milk bath,
dipping myself in Bastet's bloom

(august 11, 2016)

Baptism

your eyes burn steady embers,
ancient redwoods give of themselves
so that hands can hold, tighter, tighter,
push into the soft parts, smooth wood
on salty-sweet flesh,
                                       not a meditation
on oneness, an absence of its opposite,
a dog lying in the sun, that sort of thing
that kind of truth

in a yellow room i glow orange for you
poppies in my throat,
rosehips, apricot thighs,
our youth

(august 11, 2016)

your clay hands, and their golden keys, pressing through palms,
or are they mine? unlocking, memorizing, mirroring, mired in the
pain of forgetting, we're tearing down buildings to make something
new, you, you are mine, surely, shamefully I say this because I can't
make claims, not yet, not now, not when the winds of uncertainty pass
over our solid and soft cocoon

these poems are quiet raindrops on the roof,
the light inside your neck
warms my wet tongue
when we're inside,
alone in your room

(august 12, 2016)

Baptism

Pyromaniac posing as an idle gardener I'm partnering with Life, pouncing on it like I can't dig my claws any deeper into its lengths

(august 12, 2016)

allow, allow, allow - you will have all that you seek because the seeds spring from inside, nothing comes to you it comes from within, kindred, make a home between your hips and feel the pages in their hands, your hands, don't you see the pictures? already, the stars' light hits us from far away. doom and gloom deranges, and wishes do come true.

a hymn for our healing, write me a rhyme, something to bite on, fingers at night. the swans go about their pairing, thoughtless and fine, so why can't I, why can't I. there are plenty twists and turns in the maze, but only one exit. we will get there in time.

a warm drink that I down, a cabinet for my trinkets. a story that does not end, now, only barely written

(august 14, 2016)

Baptism

always imploring, perhaps I need a few more angels on my case, a life-vest, so that I may stay afloat, because what is before me becomes blurry when the tides of times past overcome me, because you are you, because what we wish for is always just beyond the veil, if only we can close our ears to those fatal whisperings

because what came before is just a memory. and there is always another autumn

(august 14, 2016)

Crowley

let my body rest on the shore, coughing up saltwater tears aged by the moon, the clouds protect me from that inevitable sun, the one that will hold me, the one that will keep me warm. I'm being lifted up, though it's only beginning, brought up to my place, ascending, ascending. let's see what winning feels like, let's follow our dreams, bathe in Jupiter's light, become what we'll be

(august 14, 2016)

Baptism

we'll stick all ten fingers on the cactus needles, we'll breathe the hot sun, in in in and expel outwards all that holds us back, there are a few things, our own fear being the only one. curse all limitation we didn't choose for ourselves, god didn't put a limit on wildflowers, they grow where they please. how they please.

(august 15, 2016)

Mother of all mothers, my flower in the dark, cleanse me in your saccharine waters, in a dream at a dark crimson bar I asked for white wine, buttery yellow

Brutal killer, Nuit, reach your hands into the eternal nocturnal where thorns fall away, we sway, like evergreens in a storm and of course the sun speaks in the roots of our feet but to those images that we scorn we must devote a funeral pyre far out at sea

eyelashes, eyelashes we all fall down, into graves so our bodies can be lost and be found

empty, yes, but full of new life. what surrounds you is fated what kills you is kind

(august 15, 2016)

Baptism

the night covers us all with unclenched hands

sorrow allowed, let us not pretend

second-skin purple satin, you robed me in silk you held my hands in your reverie

at a circular table I talked to you, in divine crystals we gazed, we were but two candle flames, young and waiting

we chant still, but quietly, death seems to roar but birth whispers gently

(august 15, 2016)

Crowley

she said Become Me, dark red becomes you, victorian sense and opium dens, beware, you are not of this time. maybe your power collects dust in the past let it enfold you, fingers following spells let it undo you, you may need to pass through the spider's web but don't let it stop you,

surrender, you are willing, and we see you. let it seize you.

(we were once children, too, and when we crawled from the black hole we were fearful, ravished though we find you we aren't near you, we are in you)

(august 15, 2016)

Baptism

I STOOD AT YOUR DOOR AND COMPELLED YOU
no you needn't invite me in I adore you,
see in my eyes the space shaped like you
I implore you, blink twice remember where you're from
I can't tell you, how primordial you really are,
I commend you, child, sister, sorceress, sinister siren
oh how the oceans speak of you, silent, in your
solitude you will reach us, be mindful. written in your skin
we will find you.

(august 15, 2016)

they say we aren't divine because we are diviners

last night I dreamt pretty words but only these stayed:

'Pan's fortune,
rose-garden'

adrift in the thick blood that pours from hungry mouths,
on a full moon cut yourself open with one beloved thorn,
steady, steady, the dark will contain you, walls around a
secret garden

sweet smoke and rolling waves, forest green damp leaves
we leave the ivy but trail the warm earth, lips sewn shut like
we've seen too much, close your eyes and you'll see it, too,
shadowed groves, my father with hooves

(august 16, 2016)

Baptism

a return to Catholicism, wooden pews, song-books, sorrow,
the hands of a child clasped in prayer, eyes squeezed shut oh
how he hears me, he still does, my voice booms louder, phone
to my ear he feels my warm wet breath. sorrow, the same as love,
a room only made for us, the air orange, scent citrine and I'm falling,
there is only this room.
there is only one crucifix, though my gods understand, they acquiesce
for wholeness, holiness of any kind, and though the dirt is my deed the
heart has its hallows, altars old and ancient, we will destroy that which
destroyed us, did not see us, do not deny the evils of men bent on revile,
for we seek only beauty, not malaise or terror. leave that to the forest, it
knows what to do with it, fertilizer, fecundity, furor

fail me not, oh saints, though I do not know your names, you know mine

duality will not erase my piety and you will not erase my soul, I am not

wrestling with the angels, but with devils dressed in white and gold

(august 16, 2016)

berries about to burst,
berries ripe, deep dark purple
set against dark green vines,
this is where we're at.

August.

we would swim in it if we could,
juice, electric juice,
on this Aquarius full moon,
stars in the sky shine light on
blood-red baths and shining eyes
peach nectar peach poison, drown
ourselves in opulence, candor, candied
craze, I'm cautious, but I'm plunging

lower

lower

lower

into dirt, dissolution
fall brings destruction
so we can be pure

pure as night

(august 17, 2016)

Baptism

full of it, overflowing, almost, but we'll let our pure juices push against thin walls of skin until it's so dark we must give it a taste. and then we will know sweetness, and then we will know ourselves

(august 17, 2016)

we keep looking through old photos like there's something to save, a hand to hold tight before the wind takes us forward, womanhood isn't something you arrive at it's something you return to

(august 18, 2016)

Baptism

light green moss, white sage
carefully place your future into mine,
intertwined all along, late summer rain
makes way for something more, softly,
soulfully, solely - skin sewn back on
taught, prologue, dedication, perhaps -

people always say that you'll know
well, I know

(august 19, 2016)

Berry Juice and Holy Water

foamy sea waves, sea snakes
white, black, blooming, powerful,
quaking inside the womb, I'm
looking for mine,

let the evergreen dew touch my arms,
slide, downward and pool between my
thighs, hopeful, ready, feeling, friendly,
 fool, on the cliff with my knapsack,
helpful belongings, wild eyes and a
child's laugh, softer hands fearless hearts
 fool, one to plant seeds on rainy days
and wait for the bloom

(august 19, 2016)

Baptism

an open field, big enough for this love,
in a white dress I will feel you - layers and layers
of yes's and I do's, years of wondering who, fragrant
flower posey dream, purposeful planning, harvest after
green

in every parallel universe I am smiling

(august 19, 2016)

Amber Leaves and Cautious Teeth

ripening, three words or three letters,
nails grown long my favorite things
showered in it, hands against plum walls
hold me forever, harmless words,
haunted, two birthmarks, let me please you,
perfumed wrists and romantic trysts,
twice, two of cups, touchless and touched

(august 19, 2016)

Baptism

easily frightened, pressed against the precipice,
we are waiting, charged, moonlight water, moonlight heart,
lay me down to rest, hair hugging sweet grass, in a frock,
hands interlocked, eyelids pressing. sleepy beauty, simply
kiss me, caress and release me, from stories untold. filed
away in briefcases we burnt the room, eulogy for my
sadness, funeral for the old

(lower, lower, so she cannot speak, her words are white ghosts, her eyes cannot see)

(august 19, 2016)

i will be kinder, so the world can be kind to me
(sigh, rose, child, again)

(august 19, 2016)

Baptism

bruised fruit bitten into twice,
(love's flags waving, take one more bite)

(august 19, 2016)

is it raining everywhere? or just on my legs, tender-footed start again, prepare, prepare.

(august 19, 2016)

Baptism

EARTH MOTHER

the umbrella under which we stand,
ever-shouting, reigning, allowing

you are the one that lays me down under old trees
ancient, falling, kiss me, surrounding,

black light in my eyes remind me of the other side
candles, daemon, blood

(august 19, 2016)

elderberries in the night you are mine, crystal glass and chandelier, sing me to sleep when you are near

(you are all that I am so enshrine me, temple to the bloody muddy goddess, birth me and cradle all my parts, tectonic plates converge and this mountain is our shrine, scale it and remember how we move and collide)

(august 19, 2016)

Baptism

in the farthest room of the house, down an unlit hallway, lives the heartbreaker. we hear the echoes at night and assume they're outside, we hear his nails on the wall and the smashing of glass, we don't cover our ears because we are wondering: should we be afraid?

(august 20, 2016)

every morning I wake up and the ladybug has moved
jupiter's fingers touch every room of my soul as I swallow solitude's water
I remember that analysis is useful only when it lends me to god
and when my heart begins to ache I can always go back to sleep

it's important to knock on each door and see who lives inside
we must keep track of the residents, know their faces and their names

at night I whisper it all and he puts his ear to the wall -
he nods his head, and I, the creation, nod too

(august 21, 2016)

Baptism

I'm watering my plants now.
when we lie in the dirt we cling to the earth we are afraid of what will come
as if our eyes would open in a crowded room and though it looks like our dreams
it does not feel like something that belongs to us

I wouldn't want that

small steps, shuffling shoed feet on dusty trails, checking for familiarity,
embarking on something new but it must be old.

(august 21, 2016)

two homes now.

a ranch out in the desert. nighttime, owls. the light from the stars is old, in a way that is perceptible. smoke rising from the rooftop, it's a slow process, but we're burning it down. this once was a hideaway, with its dungeons, its delight. far-removed so that we could heal. red carpet, no lights. no light at all.

*

a real home. red slippers, wood. velvet robe, descending hair, we walk slower now, we must learn to breathe air. life in paintbrushes, life in writing, life in books, life in beauty. a womb. fissures that produce new growth. lightbeams. open windows gentle breeze, perfume. misty eyes mists of the future. time will tell the story of the bard, and we will sit down and tell our story, too. we do not notice the ticking of the clock, we only hear the murmuring of our hearts.

(august 21, 2016)

Baptism

it stopped raining
an adolescent came banging on glass doors
thorns thorns thorns held her back from me
she was Lilith in jeans she was adored and abhorred

wholeness, scattered. referential, it matters

her bloody hands. her bloody hands...
the screams are silent, lost her voice long ago
trembling in a body that begged for betrayal,
or so the story goes. my eyes go blank when I tell it
scratched on my tombstone, epitaph or epithet:
 dirty rose

the girl first killed,
her body dragged through the forest,
nature unto nature
her hair, her hair...

(august 21, 2016)

a messenger, a message sent, satellite mind, beating bleeding heart.

they'll come for me they said, nearby always, rest your head on your pillow, in your light blue cocoon, womb, child, children.

the musty scent of old books pleases like the perfume we would always wear, crack the pages open and read your story as it unfolds

you were a weary traveler worried about mirages when really an oasis had found you, unfurl here, we need you.

(august 22, 2016)

Baptism

to love a free life:
in earnest fear we uproot ourselves, as tulips we walk to the edge of our garden, peer out, see the others, industriousness, commitment, but we do not leave the garden. we stand on our roots, never allowing them to sink deeper, because no one else is planted.

we cry for what we will say, how to explain, living as a stranger here, "everyone's from somewhere else" yes but who remembers, but me, and some others. my guide here on earth is of the angels, and I the stars, but who else surrounds but those of cardboard houses, dreamed to be true.

thank you for the rain. it encloses the house so that I may remain.

eyes always on the outside, while I dream of rosebush and fountain. it is all around me.

the way the lizard loves the storm, and all other things. that is how I am.

"you must be" sit me down and be stern, I am tired of making masks.

the lizard hunts, the lizard naps.

(august 22, 2016)

and perhaps I found a family on Earth, the artists, who lived all around me, and I did not notice them encircle me, in likeness. in kindness, read our stories, know our lives. you are one of us

(august 22, 2016)

Baptism

blushed skin and oceanwater veins,
I will collect small pebbles and jewels
until my palms are heavy, spark like my
eyes, sparkle like my heart. do you feel
the gentleness in me? and will you be kind?
nothing to protect it, as if I'm made of water
the magick I possess stems from this, and only
this. sacred heart, sinful rebellion. suitors upon
suitors and I only call your name, castles twenty
leagues below sea our honeymoon villa, I am a
mermaid for you, see my excitement bleed through
into my scales, siren's song but I will not kill you, I will
let us breathe Light.

(august 22, 2016)

we pressed our heart between parchment musty and perfumed, is it a fall breeze coming to raise me up, crawling out of coffins, the Real me, long since buried, but ready to begin again.

as if my bones are made only of words, my soul a carousel of summer days, fading into summer nights, every evening a light is born, some candle, a promise

and we carry it with us, into autumn estates, a young girl hides in an unused greenhouse, where the vines can enclose her. between these four walls her imagination is real and it's all there is. alpha or omega, coming or gone, the more we talk to the other side the more we become.

you in a sweater. us in the marsh of what we will become

me, an old woman, looking back on all that I've done

(august 23, 2016)

Baptism

the corpse flower bloomed and what crawled out?
angels upon angels, the light of new hope -
angels upon angels, the lather of french soap,
so that we may move on. put our old plans to rest,
and feed the bones to the crows, there is freedom in
remembering, there is freedom in letting go

(august 23, 2016)

I saw myself in the trees, three portraits of me staring back, solid. bobbing in the wind, knowing. each leaf an eye, each eye a word - they wait with mouths closed, waiting to see if I know, too

(august 23, 2016)

Part II

in our mania we unroot, lifting up until something new is seen, sought,
was once to the side, a figure in a room, at his desk, writing
we'd think of him laughingly,
but he put his hands to the door and waited
waited to come out

yielding, yielding to life, but eyes sharp, penetrating
something of that fire we've already known, seen
the air of water, the expansive mind seen in subjectivity
dark corners, dark delight. he walked in dark alleys every night
until I called on him

(august 24, 2016)

who is the one that stands in the hall and opens all the doors?

constantly inviting in, peering through keyholes, caressing their hair
as they fall into my arms, oh how they fear living in the dark, they hear
the poundings at night of the other boarders, won't you save me? invite me
into the kitchen? where the child eats and the girl lays? taking another drag,
saying little. the third floor is haunting. we rarely rest and our eyes bleed out
for tears only come when someone's watching. and no one does. we stare in
mirrors and forget our names, did we ever have any? she is cruel, but you
are not.

his nails dig into my thigh as I console him. we won't be one until I'm bleeding,
too.

('dark-haired mother, listen to my sins')

(august 24, 2016)

Baptism

this is a poem about soft waves and lighthouses,
how you rise up and
I yield

(august 24, 2016)

the wife lives in the attic. the largest windows, light curtains billow and bend,
breathless, she is waiting (they all wait). her bed too small, her hands idle, restless
she moves towards the stove and remembers there's no one to cook for,
she looks out the window and wonders if there's someone to wait for

she pulls the letters from her desk and sees that they are blank,
but something was once written there. it's faint, erased, strange

her fourth finger feels light.
but her heart, oh it is full

(heavy, no, only when she hears his screams. only then)

(august 24, 2016)

Baptism

what do you want me to turn my rage into?

the winged woman with charcoaled skin broke through the window long ago
she is not of this house, she is earthly and ancient, the pain of new birth,
when you place such ideals in a violent world, we split apart both legs
destroying the womb desecrating the pagan temples and putting
crosses in their place

she left. she left long ago.
and will she return for her young protégé,
the woman in the woods, just sixteen,
don't you remember?
we wore black for a week

(august 24, 2016)

three ladybugs three dreams,
we saw a mother with three children
and we stood and stared in awe

so much of me is still young like
we're growing backwards, back to
the moment of our birth, so that we
can stay true, true true true.

in the river I'm
young mother
young bride

(august 25, 2016)

Baptism

we will always have our dungeons, our place of permissiveness.

the nymph in the woods glows rose-gold but in her flesh there is abandon to all things immoral, dark matter, violence, blood-shed

she sits by the river and takes down the dam

(august 25, 2016)

if they name an asteroid after me, it will represent:

a woman who is herself. a woman who writes. a poet. a sexual woman. a priestess. an artist. a soul-keeper. a woman.

a poet. a sexual woman.

(august 25, 2016)

pleasure became my compass
pleasure became my being

'I'm in a constant state of arousal; not always sexual, sometimes poetic, sometimes religious'

when we are united with our truths there is a queer feeling of surprise, when we find our destination on the map we are relieved and also astonished at how obvious it is.

(august 25, 2016)

we won't pick the berries until the very last moment, not until they're almost too ripe -
just as I let you lay between my legs just awhile longer,

(august 25, 2016)

Baptism

my ember-eyed man
musing in bed it stays in my head
I will walk with you for a hundred years,
and so there is no rush,
my fingers say it for me

(august 26, 2016)

I read of the woman emptied out, atrophied,
the devoured mother,
and perhaps I am her, too,
putting my hands up 'stop!'
no, I will not do that for you,
no, I will not feel guilt

no, no
,no

a page from a magazine, ripped out at fourteen
'WHY NO SHOULD BE YOUR FAVORITE WORD'

(august 26, 2016)

Baptism

poems become prophecy

in a shroud of tears 'no no no'
angels cover me with your wings-
I'm in need of protecting

in the night we stood with our feet in the water-
and I understood the title,
'in an ocean of my own making'
we must lay, the water thickens into a
gel, an embryo, 'i just need to be alone' to
gestate. we built a womb.

when persephone arose from the tombs she found her mother's temple burnt down

(august 27, 2016)

we were once sea goddesses
we once roamed for days and days
and poseidon stopped looking and we
were
free

(august 27, 2016)

Baptism

kiss me through the open window;
girl of light and hope and promise
you seem far away but you are near
remind me of what this is all for

grab me by my collar and pull me out,
I will fall to the floor, four stories down,
break every bone they no longer hold
me up. new body new hope.

(one room, one house. guards at the door, I'm never coming out)

(august 27, 2016)

we sprinkled salt in a circle around everything that matters,
and from the dirt in the center the witch arose
sun-lit sanguine hair salty skin,
the protector. the creator.
my sin

(august 27, 2016)

Baptism

we dove into the blood not knowing where it would take us
with eyes closed shut we swam below something,
and came out the other side blinking,
and what did we find, but Atlantis,
our past, burnt the pages, our future
begged for some missing ingredient
the solace of belonging, the source of
our believing, the fates, the fates, please,
bear our message: our message is this:
we exist. we exist. there are others like you
who feel the missing key, we are out here,
shining, believing. this exists. the magick in
your veins, the clock ticking. we exist, we exist.
that is all we need to say.

(august 27, 2016)

in a boat we sat on damp floorboards playing with dolls,
flickering eyes flickering hearts,
salt in our pores salt in our nose,
we are ready. there is only the waiting
my humming tells them where to go,
and we do not go slow, it is the pace that
will get us there. we see it off in the distance
in my ear he whispers what I'll become,
how when my foot touches sand their whole world
will shatter, no, no, do not be afraid. some things go
so we can start over. in the city square you will wander,
as the light of your soul yellows dark walls, as the people cry
in their old homes, for what they've forgotten, for what they've
become. you will bring the rain. the mountains will bring their
sympathy, and flowers will bloom. shaking from crying they
will be emptied out. the body's made of love and not much
else, the body's made of love.

as you climb through the hills you will grow larger,
until you stand at the top, statuette. reminder, devotion.
and the rest of you will float on, and you will sit in your
home, knitting stories, fairytales, something. something
they can hold

it is foretold

grow steady, now, with the solid oak
and listen to the beating organ
when it tells you to love

(august 28, 2016)

Baptism

we shut the door on the woman crying long ago
and only now, do we put our ear to the door,
as we sit on our knees, and see what it all
was for

(august 28, 2016)

my hands, soft enough,
soft like mud, lay them on my
face to cradle my thoughts,
the swirling storm, we can love
it, too, leave an offering for the
goddess setting my crops aflame,
I will heed your warning, Desire,
desire, push your hand through
the rose-bushes despite the
thorns, you may come out
skinless, you may come out
sore. say his name twice, and
if it slips out another time, like
a spirit in the night, know what
will return in the morning will be
thornless and bright

(try as you might, try as you might darling, you can't put up a fight)
(you were always the goddess in white. eyes closed waiting for sight)

(august 29, 2016)

Baptism

is it only the trees and the mud that love the storm?
when I lie in the creek I am holy, whole
as long as I can sink deeper, I won't fear
falling, tripping over the same rock that
caught my toe before. maybe I'll feel the
hand made not of bone, but wicker, grab
my waist and take me home, earthdweller,
you're evaporating, each swan cries for
heaven, each dove in the sky's a
temptation

(hold me here, hold me here, hold me down)

(august 29, 2016)

I guess I dove into the water knowing I wouldn't sink,
but float

(august 29, 2016)

Baptism

on a clear morning I went to the desert with all my belongings,
and I left them amongst the mountains, washed my hands in
the river, and walked home

(august 29, 2016)

In an empty house I sang like a child,
and my voice called forth the maiden
gold and green, as she flitted down the stairs
she could not bear to wait, locked up in towers
and braids, it was in her dissolution that she
found freedom, the pleasure of the plains,
the grass calls her name, her fingers kiss the
blades, on her knees she reaches the pinnacle,
clicking her boots against nine pentacles, pages
turn too fast as she skips ahead, and she digs a
hole but not for a grave, she plants herself and
it is saved

(august 29, 2016)

Baptism

bugs make homes in dark damp places where we never poke our fingers
my throat was one of them, the seer saw him, and laughed
and so as I sang I coughed up blood and a homely beetle,
and my heart beat fast as it met my brain

(august 29, 2016)

we peeled the history books open and read about the collapse of one empire, long-standing but corroding, as the empress wept chaos ensued and the knights fled, they were happy to leave, and she was happy to see the end.

and a girl set off on a journey, dreaming of building an empire of her own, far off past the forests, surrounded by the faeries, with towers in the sky high enough to reach the stars, and deep lakes where the mermaids sang their songs

yes, if we could create our own world... if we could rule here on earth, our hair would grow longer and our eyes would shine bright. the golden age of lying down and creating all that you are

(august 30, 2016)

Baptism

at all times the woman is rising from the black flames. in a dream my friend went missing and we formed a circle to find him. as I entered the middle ground I prepared myself for what was to come, would Lucifer slip through the open door? the door in my back, enter and you'll find a winter's past, my body nailed to an upside-down cross. perhaps she hasn't found her glory. rebirth is not climax, it's restoration. and when we reach the midheaven, which fallen angels will shriek and moan, my mothers with milk hands, they pull at new growth. last night I saw my wings covered in soot, bigger than I supposed. love and a knife.

she's still counting bodies she's still shielding sugary hearts, and while I sit upon the tree in the orange glow of a green room, she bows to me, too. heaven won't erase me, we make this world our red sea, this I do for you.

(august 31, 2016)

an eclipse of the way we used to do things, the past in shadows. only we know those days are gone, we stand upon the highest step, looking back, as the low flames hug and roll, stale air from their mouths but we know where the wetness lies. our heavy dress couth and containing, we sprinkle the ashes of an old body above the remains. eye contact with the new moon making love with the maiden, we understand. and finally our back to it, and a whole army to greet us. we weep on our knees, for we have never been supported so.

and they raise our flags, in pride and in prairie, and their shouting drowns out all that I am not. a million flags, the red of our home. the red of our becoming. craftswoman amongst the wood softened by a husband's hands, writing, writing, writing. wrestling, with the poets that couldn't eat of this.

(september 1, 2016)

Baptism

perhaps we did not know, as we took the plunge, that we would return. came back the same, but stronger - we thought we'd need a shell, but once we crawled upon our stomachs through the ivy and brine, we came out skinless. and now we sit on a cloud, nightmares at night ask us to come down, but for the sake of us all, we will not. and I see her in old photos of soft-haired women I do not know, remembrance, rustling the leaves, an omen, my bible, my loss.

in the place where the cliff dropped a story was born, more roses, and eros, his wings the whole of our fingers. dust to dust they said and I kissed her grave. we did not see the new blossoms but they raise me up. we're still the dark sea but why not the warm hearth, too. the wet leaves below me, rich soil and the moon. happiness for one girl, far beyond the bloom

lay me down and become a library, Lust, Love, Laurel, saint of the immoral. I hope to become a gateway, to what I've sequestered

(september 1, 2016)

riches and riches and gold dripped in oil, hades won't hide from me what spills from my soul, soil rich like chocolate cake, lustrous and looming, my life is improving, molten lava flows thick and we know what we're about. a dragon upon her coins, castles aplenty, purposeful planning. let me daydream in the second house, as the onlookers come closer, their eyes through the windows. secrecy, oh secrecy, I wanted you back. from the other side of the door I could create - fiendishly, foolishly. nature's folly. the nymph lives amongst the ruins, and there is only the forest, and those that wander through

(september 1, 2016)

Baptism

terracotta home walls strong the womb we called out for, my home my mother, place your hands on mine and they turn earth-brown, too, tethered like sapling roots to the ground or an anchor, the oldest oak's trunk. the roots have been there all along, waiting for us to sit upon them after a long walk in the forest. do you see in my green eyes the sea, do you melt a bit when you jump in, mud, mud, mud. clay homes, no walls. I bent in the river and sifted for gold, your reflection in the morning light was enough. three clay pots, and the forests within them

in the water I love you, in the water we're home

(september 5, 2016)

perhaps it's in the honesty, in the Word, spellbooks and fishhooks, what we reel in swims within, and spreads its wings. blinded by the feathers, soft on the eyes, there remains but one spark of light. and that's all that we are, truly, this one small thing. may it be our eyes, our hands, our words. may we pray beneath it, our stars, our moon. calm as the sea on a cloudless day, calm as can be. and full, every molecule infused with the berries of life. the ocean, the night. we are always right.

(september 5, 2016)

Baptism

wild eyes and fading neon lights, our mouth stretched wide our eyes aglow, sharp brightness, maenad child. where does it come from? we ask. out from the genie bottle, it is little leaves, first shy bloom. not shy at all. excited delighted, the fire within. furnace keeps burning one match is enough. she's tough, like the weeds that keep growing. phosphorescent, leaning, chant with me now - this life is divine

(september 6, 2016)

hands in the night fright dissolves away, open mornings green tea oceans, coral cactus

(september 7, 2016)

Baptism

in the sunless forest I hid, in the cabin wooden and wooded, untouched and wandering, virgin snow and solitary confinement, cut off the loose branches and find your belonging. there is only the circle, and the square of these walls. in here all things are allowed so long as they sprout from the dark promised night, perilous virtue and solemnous fright. fortune, my friend we've, been on a journey, a midnight stroll, merciless searching, we'll end it all. and I will lay in the lake of my desire fulfilled, as the trees tell my story, and the fae dance their fall

(september 9, 2016)

the sparkle is here, waiting, as the light lifts on the river, as the twilight closes my eyes, as the redwood veins say remember. the veil of peace descends even as my legs thrash about, but someone holds them down so I can see. and birds come in pairs and I say don't mind me, I'm just believing. in something already formed, as the sun smiled upon waking. as a path that keeps going, if I just keep walking. and the white heat of the heart is there, reinforcing, as I rest in my sailboat, prepared for a death.

wash away, oh savior, how far we have come. wash away our worries for we should have none

the elixir of peace, place on my tongue

(september 11, 2016)

Baptism

in a trunk of treasures I lay like a porcelain doll, frayed edges, soft hair, lips moving I share: the value of small love, that bursts through the seams, makes life a dream, to hold and to be. a story on my palms, the river and its voices. off through the palms, in dark and damp houses. so I slumbered through morning, as the ship carried me your way. and woke up at dawn, to the ocean's last day.

(september 11, 2016)

living proof: the seashells are in our bag, three for keepsake, and so when we stare into the sea we are not lost in it, bobbing away, breasted and brave, curled up concubine caressed by the waves, keepsake secrets, floating, floating, the longest string tying us back, and we can relax, knowing the eagle sees when we do not.

mermaid castle, secret homes. saccharine, sacrilege, suck my fingers and taste - there are two spaces, and we must lay our head in the other. let the aliens caress your temples, and tell you where you're from. heaven, the horses, where do they run

(september 13, 2016)

Baptism

two portraits, twins, angel fins and foolish things, folly is infallible or so they say. rose-picked pockets, silken strands, on our sense we stand, flour and grain, and floating feet. her mumbling teeth, a smooth melody, the twelfth house on the left, and its singing balcony. you must wake us up, lest we sink into sand, heavy and wet with ocean powder. its salt in our hands, its salt in our hair.

could we breathe fall air and its cradling, custodians to our flowering, let each layer die. until what is useful arises, until the cats surround and the softness surrends

(september 13, 2016)

an ocean blanket and the seashell on my ear, howling as the moon ripens, echoes of the past won't stop me now, songs we stopped playing. and the sun breaks the current so that my body is mine, so that we align, so four becomes two and softness compels you and the sea urchins throw their rocks until we. wake up

the rusting leaves will hold me, the promise of more. we are bedbound and ridden, and the heart's the one healing. the butterflies arise during visiting hours, to tell of our becoming, and to smile. and in the green we find hope, as the earth sustains, and the red robins go about their day

(september 14, 2016)

Baptism

at the very center a table is being set, in the orange glow all is known, and it is only the electric storms outside that keeps us from seeing. onward, onward, out - we are not foolish for loving, we are all that is. and as we lay our heads on the ground we are warm, and a guardian unlocks the door, and we must accept the open. we must open and open and let the breeze blow in, as the chest rattles and the dust is sent to the wind. we are seen, and held, by the safety of the orange and brown glow

(september 14, 2016)

open house, open air, let the stars fall in, and we will drown in it, in the obviousness, in the heart to heart. in the light that shines, in the hope that enfolds. and we'll seal the envelope, with a thank you note inside, and send it to the universe, where this all began

(september 14, 2016)

Baptism

cinnamon and butter my hair past my shoulders, the brown of my birth and the warm warm earth, the waterfall and its sighing, we're learning and complying, sometimes the soul must do some crying, if we want to come clean. not much to admit, but the scars we can't see, I don't feel them today. I set myself free.

(september 16, 2016)

you don't need to listen to that song again, our hands aren't made of ash and our heart's not hidden. do this for me, please, lay down all the thoughts you've collected over time, just lay them on the ground and walk on by

before, before, before, something from before. rest assured. the healer is stronger than the wound, and you, too, can remain whole

watch as the waves smooth down the sand, watch how it's all erased

smooth, smooth, succulent.

(september 16, 2016)

Baptism

I'm opening the door - are you ready? the light does not blind, it caresses, like the transfer of a flame, from match to wick, to morning dew's kiss. capable and cunning, the witch's long nails as they scratch spells into wax, and she designs, and she desires, and we all bow to her, that terrible witch woman.

small socked feet on soft-wood floors, supple turning of the day into noon, we follow the drums through the hallway of our house, mourning, the cry and the shake, happiness for happiness' sake, and we let it beat our blood, there is truth for the taking, there's a shine in your eyes -

I stand by the door and I trust. I stand by the door and I must.

(september 17, 2016)

I pray to the shadow of the desert, its green aurora, its totality - let the darkness descend as I cradle this arrow, we bled so we could see, what is inside of me? and what is purple, what vanquishes and what careens, I can't give it up, when it's the only thing that means

and I was a dancer in that valley, and I'm a dancer in this room. Exhume - and let it jewel your throat, the rubies of our being, tall tan and thinning, sitting and sitting, the frog tumbles off my tongue as you see the blood behind my cheeks. A Wail of centuries, let the centaurs stumble upon my stomach and I'll bleed out more, left in the forest, left to grow

to rot, the moister the soil the deeper our breath, caught by a tree with something to speak, Do This For Me, if not for you then think of me, too, the message is in the rings, circles and circles and precious pink things, the inside of my lip

me and my mausoleum, and the daemon, too, we won't fear fallen leaves, and the dead won't rise. leave salt in the shape of a mouth, and take this with you. the shadow of the desert, its green aurora.

exhume... exhume... exhume...

(september 17, 2016)

Baptism

the woman dining alone, the moment of separation, making reparations and seeding plans. flee to the window, unfurl. tigers with claws that keep safe, and a whispered desire: 'You see when I was young I...' no, no, I, am a swimming stream of this thing, drop a coin or two in if you're wishing, out comes the tar now, turn her on her side. tuck the playing spirits in so they won't pull at our skirt, praying, eyes watery, decaying.

we will dance around the fire, the night's cool air our lover, the whole dark sky our savior, ride this, die for this, childish for this, we are praying. and we want, too. desirous and drifting, we'll catch one or we're kidding, we're sifting through sand and unbelieving in time, we are folded

and we're asking, I open my mouth and tilt my head back. my tongue stays wet, and we are completed.

(september 17, 2016)

no more of the crumbling city. we only live in plains and gardens, forests when our eyes are heavy. life is not a hunter and we are not the deer, place your hands in mine and see the love in my eyes, you are not the deer. trust, trust, as the water falls, as your hand fits in mine. trust, trust, and let it all fall away. notice this, the fighting lion that knows the other way. my body needs a renovation - gut out the interior, and paint the walls

light blue and lullabies, when we wake we have chosen, when we wake we realize

(september 18, 2016)

Baptism

we fell asleep with our feet in the water, fire's water, and when we woke we were high, swirling, closer to the cloud from which my raindrop fell, fooling and foiling the society in which we grew. yes if I could only be these leaves, growling, if I could only be the top-most branch, unwavering. we see the plains of least resistance, and topple down, we mustn't miss it, the wild cat craving its jewel

and the posing red flowers and the lavender hours, we were given the seeds, the soil, the rain - while your left hand questions the right hand plants. and plant we shall, purposeful planning, my overlord in the stars, this life we are granting

grow... grow... grow...

(september 18, 2016)

dislocation, the soul's sabbatical, perhaps weaving the silkscreen sky, creating a new web for us, here on earth, coughing up dirt, in wholeness I find you in wholeness I'm home, but we must roll ourselves in it, the discordant parts, glass in skin, captured butterflies, a piece of me dies, as I caress it

and prick my fingers - could the blanket of sleep cure it, or is it the startled awakening of Truth Truth Truth Truth - the angels lay the pages before me, force my eyes wide. Read this and Know. Every day is a destination, and fullness is already here. Here, here, hear... we don't whisper in the night we

are so silent that you can finally hear, your own soul's titterings. your own heart's flutterings. and your desire's moans

(september 19, 2016)

Baptism

we won't leave the tree's hollow, not while there's still time. lay me down on dried petals so I can think. the healer's daughter, her blood-stained hands.

but I am still open - as the dandelion gives of itself and the rain, the rain. wash away their sins in the river bend, pull out the poppies and pretend - you know when you soften your mind and dreamily live? lucidity and lover's luck, nature's honey we can't get enough. up here we are steering, down below we are sleeping

and it's deep, this eternal sleep, as we return whence we came. the soil's heart, our mother's veins. push and pull like the tide gone wild, we won't divert from the plan, the compass inside, encircled in tissue sapling root grime, my fecund womb, I just bloom and I bloom

up from the subway I danced, and stood in neon shine, puddles and people, my dark wetted night

(september 19, 2016)

feathered hair beauty laps at olive oil, two tigers won't tell you what it took to get here, now it's gold necklaces, cool marble steps. cautious surrender, our lips torn asunder, cherry blossom heart - let the sap ooze out. awestruck, defiant - the woman and her ecstatic vision, allow her to convulse. the throes of pain won't push the daemon out. her head on the cool wet tile, lost in waves of emotion. a thousand hands, lifting the skirt

cosmic light, cosmic duty, a cult in the sixties, a boarded up house. picking up and remembering, reflecting its ending. where do we belong. naked in the woods, a horror-struck story, witches bemoan and this dream I carry. lost worn and weary. we kiss toads and we know divinity - and for this we are loved

by the big-eyed and faerie, lick our ankles and see us married, the poet's drenched parchment unspools and surrounds me

and it's gold, like the dust of our consignment

(september 19, 2016)

Baptism

each thick layer of skin, dermis dermis dermis, each hard bone, removed, gently, but fully, constantly, so I, the soft-celled human, can really show

(september 20, 2016)

and the deer comes out - behind cherry blossom flowers, eyes wide and waiting, frail limbs she's stepping, into another land
another land, another hope. we let ourselves start wishing. on stars, ladybugs, rope. a knot tied tight, keeping with the promise. I'm trying to be honest. open. whole

(september 20, 2016)

Baptism

I dreamt that I only wore red. Red red red red, the fire of my soul, an apple, falling into the flames. Burnt. Resurrected. Blood and prehistoric teeth

(september 20, 2016)

falling from grace, the earth mother's face, as she picks up her child and takes her away. furrowed brow, clutched to her waist, we aim to protect but could we allow -

and the veiled woman covers us with her robe - eyes accustomed to darkness close and heavily we breathe out. can I see you through black stitches?

we turn away. behold the altar and rest our heads on lost gods' shoulders. could you dazzle me in dark night's reverie, could I forget this?

interrogating the mirror, passing back and forth a ball of rotten tissue. no it doesn't feel good and when I lay my newborn body in a shallow grave it's too familiar. it's getting old.

as if I could claw my way to the other side, upon a newer day, as if to run from the flame would help me forget

(we are our own ghosts)

(september 23, 2016)

Baptism

in a moment of weakness the bones of my ribcage grow thicker, and vines begin to encircle them, oh the vines and their shadowing. my hand and its pressing, just trying to stop the bleeding

but it all pours out, the lady and her vase, watering gardens not of our choosing

and the virgin, throwing her match into its forest, and watching the flames rise,

as they do, when we're destroying

(september 23, 2016)

the masochist is the sadist in disguise, her dagger hidden behind her black robe as she drops roses on the ground, the hallowed ground of love seen from the other side of a fence. will the weight of my bones bring my legs to the floor, each night the nail moves an inch through my fist and I seem screaming for more

but the cross at my back grows thinner, as fallen angels grow familiar and the pain fails to deliver

bloodshed won't suffice we'll make no more sacrifice,

my heartstrings grow thicker,

and I am freed from this war

(september 23, 2016)

Baptism

artemis's flowers and her sixty nymphs,
aphrodite's perfume and her gasps of delight
the revolving heart between spread legs, gold
dripping respite, hands sliding on lily pads, as
naiads grasp at our ankles, in the water it
makes sense, in the water we're whole

and the bubbles of air pass by our heads,
thinking is for later, submersion is eternal,
and the infinite laughs

we are breast, plumage, arrest -
love under lune

a dark walking moon

(september 24, 2016)

one feather and its graceful descent from the sun to the shore, in our hearts we were craving in our hearts we had more.

(september 25, 2016)

Baptism

my blood and the echoes upon the pines, the things the fog speaks, the resounding and dividing, this is real and that will fall away into the earth after we're gone. only the fauns know, only the sequestered nymph. embracing the dampened bark she surrenders her heart, as if this is our last day. in the shadowy grove her desires can play, and the light of her soul gives her away

(september 29, 2016)

Crowley

the rose wasn't under glass it was right here waiting, we shook and shook and shook as fear summoned us to gaze upon that mirror, the one that tells us, you are swimming snuggly in the grooves of the golden earth, let it hold you. don't let the new moon collapse you, there is left the violet fog, the scent of the trees turning their faces. we lay in the lack of blue and we face it, the gold and brown resting on our chest

and we are encircled,
cycling,
to what we
have found

(september 30, 2016)

Baptism

I was incinerated by uncertainty, and milky hands sifted through the ash, until they found only joy. the golden locket, a small carousel, the raspberry heart, the love letter. the rest is ash. we always look for more, surely there is something else, but no, only the words carved into the floorboards - Tell Your Story. my story, my message. and the wings that brought me here

and the fool wears the locket, permits herself much. hearing the flowers, drinking the sun.

(september 30, 2016)

a heavier air - dense with the smell of tumbleweed flowers, the warmth radiating from the earth's chest, its pulse - living, living, living, our lips - dripping, dripping, dripping and the polleny haze that softens our eyes, fleshes our cheeks, permits no disguise; we fall into it, we rise. undulating restoration, let the earth grasp and shake a little. until we feel it in our spine, and we fall away

did we see, in that smile, eyes like Pan's, eyes like mine -

sunshowered youth, gasping sharp-toothed, from hell's first inferno, or Vesta's glowing hearth, oh, we've tapped into life's gold

(september 30, 2016)

Baptism

oh October, hold me -
the salted nights and the purple loom,
fascinated with shades of brown, and
the curtain closing on summer past,
in the darkness the faeries sing, as
they did at my birth, as they do around
me

(october 1, 2016)

www.ingramcontent.com/pod-product-compliance
Lightning Source LLC
LaVergne TN
LVHW041623070426
835507LV00008B/421